Jane Bull
Animals
Made by Me

DK

LONDON, NEW YORK, MUNICH,
MELBOURNE, and DELHI

DESIGN AND TEXT Jane Bull
PHOTOGRAPHER Andy Crawford
SENIOR EDITOR Carrie Love
DESIGNER Hannah Moore
PRE-PRODUCTION PRODUCER Raymond Williams
PRODUCER Ché Creasey
CREATIVE DIRECTOR Jane Bull
CATEGORY PUBLISHER Mary Ling

This 64pp Edition
SPECIAL SALES CREATIVE PROJECT MANAGER
Alison Donovan
PRE-PRODUCTION PRODUCER Rebecca Fallowfield
PRODUCER Charlotte Oliver
EDITOR Manasvi Vohra
SENIOR DTP DESIGNER Pushpak Tyagi

First published in Great Britain in 2013 by
Dorling Kindersley Limited
80 Strand, London WC2R 0RL
Penguin Group (UK)

A CIP catalogue record for this book
is available from the British Library.

ISBN: 978-1-4093-4805-4

Printed and bound in China
by South China Printing Co. Ltd.

Discover more at
www.dk.com

Meet the animals

Creating creatures

All the projects in this book will begin by telling you what materials you'll need to make it. The most essential piece of equipment is the Sewing kit – have this ready at all times. Also, shown here are other things that you'll find useful.

Sewing kit

Here are the sewing essentials – keep them collected up in a handy box.

Sewing thread

Keep an array of threads plus some other creature colours too such as black, grey and brown.

Tape measure

For measuring up your fabric when starting a project and some precision positioning.

Thimble

On big projects doing a lot of hand stitching can make your middle finger sore – use the thimble on your middle finger to push the needle through.

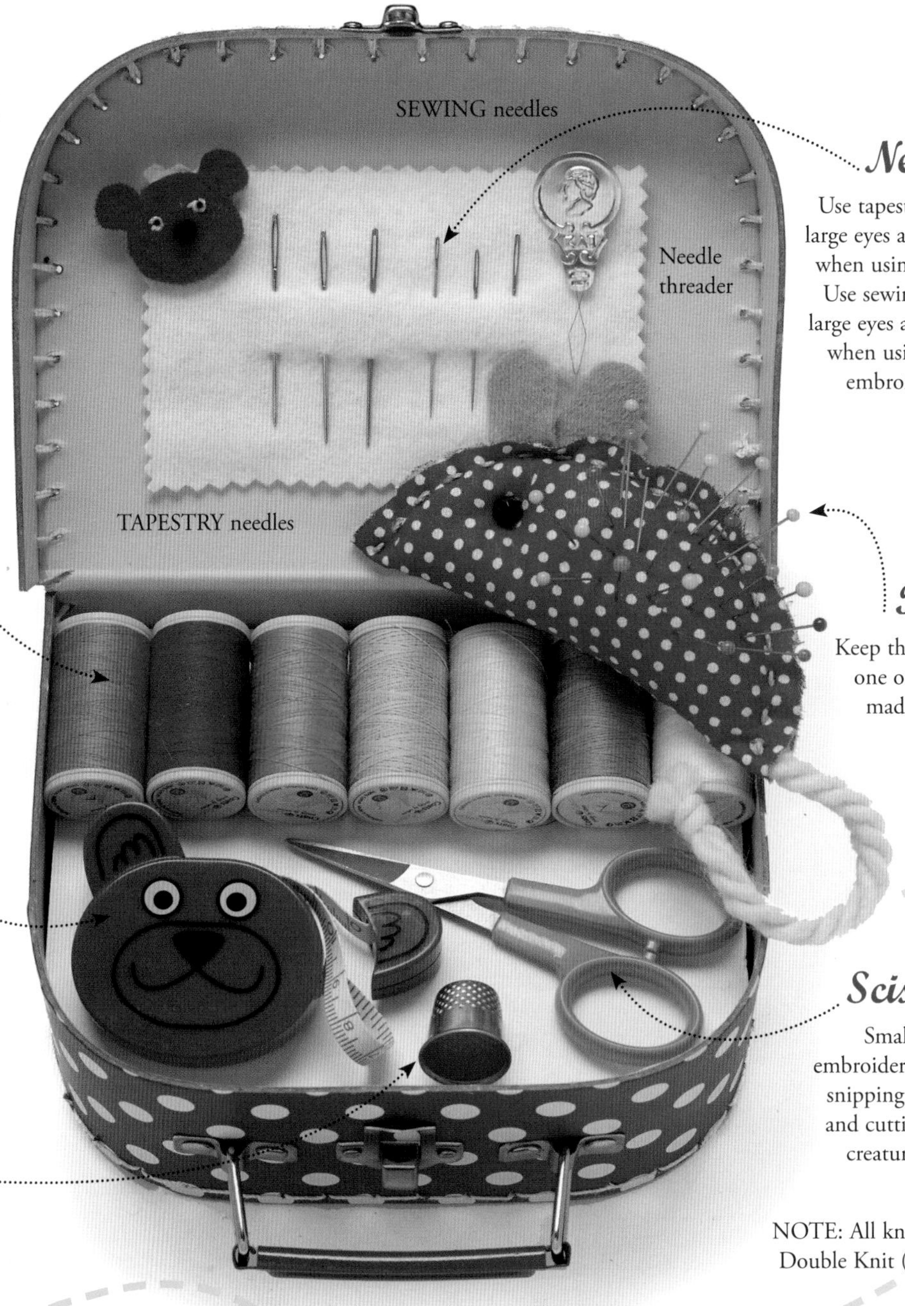

SEWING needles

TAPESTRY needles

Needle threader

Needles

Use tapestry needles with large eyes and rounded ends when using knitting yarn. Use sewing needles with large eyes and pointed ends when using sewing and embroidery thread.

Pins

Keep them to hand in one of your home made cushions.

Scissors

Small sharp embroidery scissors for snipping off threads and cutting out tiny creature shapes.

NOTE: All knitting patterns use Double Knit (DK) weight yarn

These will be useful too...

From cutting out larger pieces of fabric to stuffing your projects.

Large scissors

For cutting out templates and larger pieces of fabric these large scissors are best. It helps if the scissors are sharp as this makes them easier to use and they give better results.

Pinking shears

These scissors will prevent cotton fabric fraying because their blade is zig-zag shaped. The effect is attractive as well and can be used for decoration.

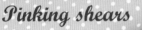

Embroidery thread

The thickness of this thread is good when you want to see the stitches. It is used for decorative stitches as well.

Felt fabric

Felt is so versatile – it's easy to shape and it doesn't fray when cut. This makes it perfect to use for tiny projects and great creature features.

Soft toy filling

This polyester fibre is used for all the projects in this book. It's very soft and can be easily worked into all the different animal shapes.

Buttons

Colourful buttons in all sizes are good for eyes and noses and noses and make great decorations.

Cosy cats

Here are a couple of contented cats –
their simple quirky shape and flat base help them
to sit quite happily together.

Little cat

Cat body

Trace over the shape to
make a paper pattern.

Cat base

1

Pin the two felt shapes together. ⋯⋯⋯

Sew the shapes together with overstitch (see page 54), leaving the bottom open.

2

Fill the cat shape from the base.

Pin the base to the body and overstitch in place.

3

Add buttons for the eyes and pink felt for the ears.

Sew on the features to finish off your cat.

Bigger cats

To make a bigger cat simply enlarge the template on a photocopier, cut out the shapes and use the copies as your paper pattern. This big cat was made by increasing the template by 200 per cent.

You will need

Cut 2 felt shapes for the body 13cm x 12cm (5¼in x 4¾in).

Sewing kit (see page 4-5), buttons for eyes, felt ears, fabric motif, and sewing thread.

Cut one felt shape for the base 10cm x 6cm (3½in x 2½in).

Pocket pets

Rover

These little critters are all made using the same basic template design. Just change ears, beaks, and snouts to create all kinds of different pals.

Basic body shape for all the pets.

Trace over the shapes to make a paper pattern. Turn to page 10 to see how.

Pinky the Pig comes to visit

How to make Rover's house

Take a large juice carton, cut it down to make a cube shape and cut out a door. Cover the sides and roof with felt.

Sit the house on a grassy felt mat.

Cut a strip of green felt with a spiky edge to create flower stalks.

Ribbit

Pinky

Cheeky

Patch

Li'l Chick

You will need

- Coloured felt – 10cm x 8cm (4in x ¼in) for each body.
- Felt scraps for noses and eyes.
- Sewing kit (see page 4–5)
- Soft toy stuffing

Rover

Red

Kitty

Tie a key ring to a length of ribbon, and stitch the ribbon to the head of the pet.

Working pets

Keep your pets as little creatures in your pockets or turn them into something. Use them as fobs for your keys or hang them on your backpack. Alternatively, sew a pin to the back and have your pets as a brooch.

Stitch a safety pin to back to make a brooch.

How to make a paper pattern

Place tracing paper over the picture on the page. Trace over each of the features separately – the basic body shape, the ears, and any other features. Cut these out and pin them to the felt. Use this method to make your big pet too.

Trace over the basic body shape, then the ears, patch, and collar.

Cut out each shape.

Use this method to make the body shape for the other pets.

How to make Rover

Use this method to make all the pets. It's easier to stitch the face and the nose on the front piece first before attaching it to the back shape.

1

Pin the paper to the felt.

Cut 2 body shapes.

Cut one of each of the ears, patch, and collar.

2

Leave an opening at the top for the filling.

Attach the patch and sew on the face.

Take one piece of felt body shape.

3

Place front and back together.

Stitch the two body pieces together using overstitch (see page 54).

4

Add the filling.

Continue stitching to close the opening.

Work the stuffing into his paws.

5

Wrap the collar around the neck and stitch in place.

Alternatively, you can use fabric glue.

6

Stitch the ears to the top of the head.

Mice made easy

Cut out a disc of pretty cotton fabric. By simply folding it in half you can create a charming little mouse shape.

Any lightweight cotton or felt fabric will work.

Cut a disc of fabric 11cm (4¼in) wide.

You will need
- Cotton fabric for body 13cm x 13cm (5¼in x 5¼in)
- Felt for ears • Beads for eyes
- Sewing kit (see page 4-5)
- String for a tail • Soft toy filling

1

Ear shapes made from felt.

Pin the fabric together.

Fold the fabric in half.

2

Sew in the ears as you go.

Sew along the edge nearly to the end.

With embroidery thread, sew in running stitch (see page 54) from the nose end.

Fill up the mouse's body.

3

Tie a knot in the end of the string.

Place the tail in the opening and sew it in place.

4

Use sewing thread to sew on beads for the eye.

Finish sewing and fasten off.

Colour mix mice

Play with the colours of fabric, felt, and thread that you use. Match them or mix them up to create some stunning clashes.

Sewing tip

When sewing on the beads for the eyes, begin by sewing one eye in place then take the needle through the fabric to the other side of the head and attach the other eye. This way the eyes will dip into the fabric.

Gift ideas

• **Brooch:** Sew a safety pin to the back of a mouse.
• **Pin cushion:** Pop in some pins and add it to a sewing kit
• **Smelly mice:** mix some dried lavender in with the filling to make a fragrant gift!

How tall are the Teds?
Little Ted stands 18cm (7in) high and Big Ted is 33cm (13in) tall.

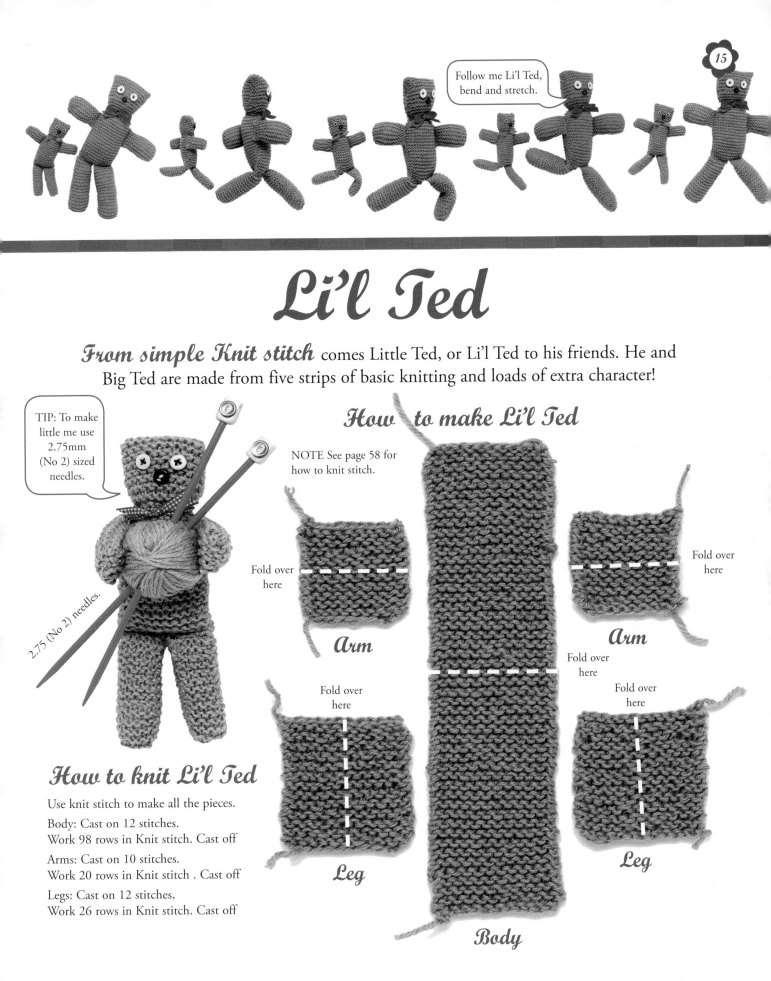

Follow me Li'l Ted, bend and stretch.

Li'l Ted

From simple Knit stitch comes Little Ted, or Li'l Ted to his friends. He and Big Ted are made from five strips of basic knitting and loads of extra character!

TIP: To make little me use 2.75mm (No 2) sized needles.

2.75 (No 2) needles.

How to make Li'l Ted

NOTE See page 58 for how to knit stitch.

Fold over here

Arm

Fold over here

Arm

Fold over here

Fold over here

Body

Fold over here

Leg

Fold over here

Leg

How to knit Li'l Ted

Use knit stitch to make all the pieces.

Body: Cast on 12 stitches.
Work 98 rows in Knit stitch. Cast off

Arms: Cast on 10 stitches.
Work 20 rows in Knit stitch . Cast off

Legs: Cast on 12 stitches,
Work 26 rows in Knit stitch. Cast off

Keep up Li'l Ted, run, step and jump.

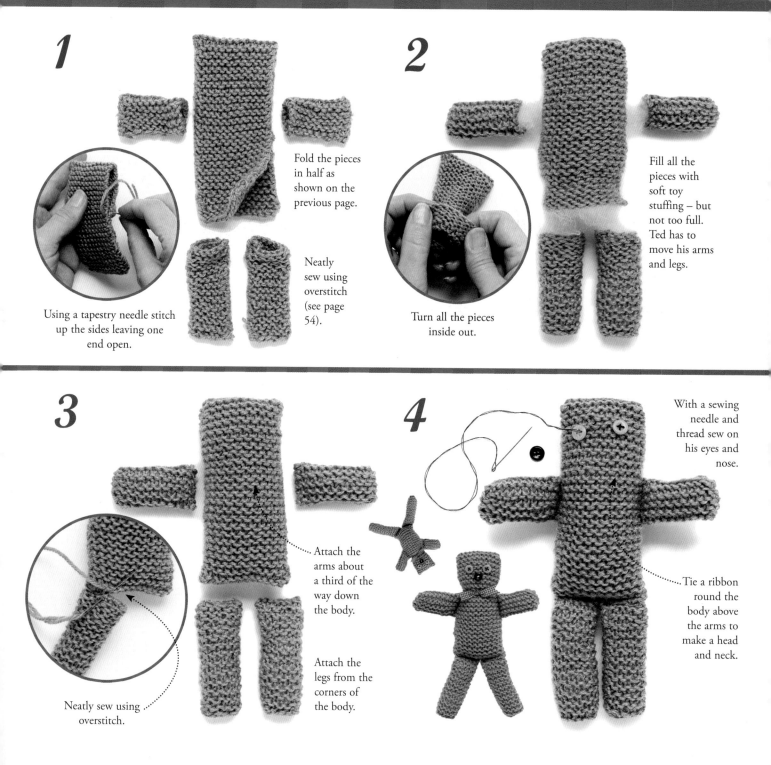

1

Fold the pieces in half as shown on the previous page.

Neatly sew using overstitch (see page 54).

Using a tapestry needle stitch up the sides leaving one end open.

2

Fill all the pieces with soft toy stuffing – but not too full. Ted has to move his arms and legs.

Turn all the pieces inside out.

3

Neatly sew using overstitch.

Attach the arms about a third of the way down the body.

Attach the legs from the corners of the body.

4

With a sewing needle and thread sew on his eyes and nose.

Tie a ribbon round the body above the arms to make a head and neck.

Steady Li'l Ted, don't go crazy...

Ta daaaaa!

For Big Ted you will need

4mm (No 6) Knitting needles
1 x ball double knit yarn
in brown.

How to knit Big Ted

Use knit stitch to make all the pieces.
Body: Cast on 20 stitches. Work 136
rows in Knit stitch. Cast off
Arms: Cast on 15 stitches. Work 32 rows
in Knit stitch. Cast off
Legs: Cast on 20 stitches, Work 40
rows in Knit stitch. Cast off.

Ted ideas

Use other colours of wool
to make Ted. He can be blue or
green or even pink! Why
not try a multicoloured Ted,
either with self-coloured yarn
or made from all your left
over yarn.

Dog's best friends

Dogs in transit. Using the fold of the fabric to make the dog's back gives these little pups a nice curvy shape. They are small enough to fit in your hand or the large ones make comfy cushions.

DOGS IN TRANSIT
handle with care

You will need

- Cotton fabric 14cm x 23cm (5½in x 9in)
- Felt scraps for ears, noses, and collars
- Soft toy stuffing • Buttons for eyes • Colourful thread for mouth • Sewing kit (see page 4–5)

How to Make Friends

1

Fold fabric

Place the edge of the paper against the fold.

Fold the fabric in half with the pattern on the inside.

Pin the paper to the fabric and carefully cut around the dog shape.

2

Sew round the shape using backstitch (see page 54)

Leave an opening for the filling.

3

Turn the dog shape right side out.

Fill up the shape and carefully sew up the opening.

Slipstitch (see page 54).

Now add the features

Eyes

Nose

Ears

Collar

Tail

Stitch the ears to the top of the head.

Stitch on a mouth using backstitch (see page 54).

To attach the nose, stitch backwards and forwards through the nose fabric and felt.

Wrap the felt collar around the neck and attach in place with the button.

Attach the tail in the same way as the nose.

Find the pattern
for Dog's best friend on page 60

Bees and bugs

Swarms of bees and bugs. Get creative with felt and blanket stitch – make the cutest bees and bugs there have ever beeeeeeen.

You will need

- Red felt 11.5cm x 16cm (5in x 6¼in)
- Black felt 10cm x 11.5cm (3½in x 5in)
- Sewing kit (see page 4–5)
- Soft toy stuffing

Use for body and base.

Pin the templates on to the felt and cut out the shapes.

Cut out the spots and eyes.

Body

Face

Base

Trace over the bug template. Cut one base in black, two body shapes in red. six spot and two eyes.

1 First, sew the features to the ladybird body.

2 Sew the base and one half of the top together. Use blanket stitch (see page 54).

Black base for bug.

3 Sew the other half of the body to the base in the same way.

4 Sew the two body shapes together half way. Add the filling.

5 Once filled sew up the opening.

How to make bees

Cut out the body shapes, face and eyes as for the spotty bugs. Make stripes out of black felt and two white felt wings. Sew on the strips before stitching together and add the wings at the end.

Knittens

These are knitted kittens — knit some stripy shapes, sew them up, add the filling until they're soft and cuddly, then add buttons for the eyes, and you have a Knitten.

You will need

- 1 x ball double knit yarn for body and contrasting colours for clothes • Knitting needles 4mm (No 6)
- Tapestry needle • Soft toy stuffing Buttons for eyes • Sewing kit (see page 4–5)

Head

Top

Sleeve

Paws

Trousers

Feet

Begin knitting from the feet upwards.

How to Knit a knitten

To make knitten's body

Use stocking stitch (see page 58).
Cast on 34 stitches in the
brown yarn.
Feet: Starting with knit stitch
work four rows.
Trousers: Change yarn colour (see page 56)
and work 13 rows.
Top: Change yarn colour and
work 13 rows.
Head: Change yarn colour and work
16 rows.
Cast off.

To make Knitten's arms

Use stocking stitch.
Cast on 9 stitches in the brown yarn.
Paws: • Make 4 rows starting
with knit stitch.
Sleeve: • Change yarn colour
and make 13 rows.
Cast off.

Knitten know-how

The secret to the Knitten's shape
is how to put it together. Join the
two long sides together, turn them
right way out and make sure the
seam is moved to the centre back.
This will be where the
legs are shaped (see page 24).

Stripy top or not?

Stripes are pretty, but your
Knitten's top will look just as
good in one colour and will be
simpler to make too. Even better
if you have multicoloured yarn
you'll get a colourful
effect instantly.

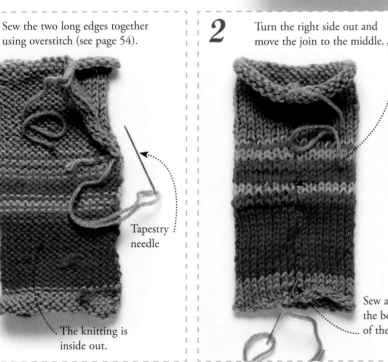

1 Sew the two long edges together using overstitch (see page 54).

Tapestry needle

The knitting is inside out.

2 Turn the right side out and move the join to the middle.

Sew along the bottom of the tube.

3

Fill the knitted pocket, but not too full.

Sew along the edge to close the opening.

4 Shaping the head

Start at the back of the head.

Use running stitch (see page 54) around the neckline.

Pull the yarn tight to gather the knitting.

Secure the yarn at the back of the head.

5 Shaping the ears and legs

To form the ear shape pinch the corner of the head.

Sew along the seam at the back of the body.

Sew at an angle to make a triangle shape

Bring the yarn backwards and forwards through the body.

Sew the arm together and turn the right side out.

6 Adding the arms

Position the arms just below the head.

Put a small amount of stuffing in the arm.

With the arm seam facing the body stitch the arm in opposition.

Cats and kittens

Cats come in all shapes and sizes. It's possible to make big and little cats by knitting different-sized rectangles. Cast on more stitches for fat cats, or deeper stripes for tall cats.

Add some buttons for eyes.

Tops and trousers

The bands of knitted colour will become the knittens clothes. The bands can be plain, or try giving them stripy jumpers like the ones shown here.

Large-sized knitten

Multicolour

If you use multicoloured yarn, you can get a variety of colours without having to change yarns.

Baby-sized knitten

Your little pony

Full of swishing tails, and manes. You can have endless fun creating a stable full of little ponies. Have a play with different colours and fabrics – go wild!

You will need

- Cotton fabric 2 pieces 20cm x 20cm (8in x 8in)
- Knitting yarn
- Tapestry needle
- Soft toy stuffing
- Felt and buttons for eyes and ears
- Sewing kit (see pages 4–5)

To make the tail

To make the swishy tail, cut 10 lengths of yarn 24cm (10 in) long. Knot them together in the middle, a slip knot works well. See page 56.

The mane is made from lengths of yarn 15cm (6in) long sewn through the fabric to form a small tassel.

Make a mouth using backstitch (see page 54).

Finish off the eye with a button stitched over the eyelash.

Once the tail is in place cut the yarn to the same length.

Find the pattern

for your little pony on page 61.

How to make your pony

1 Pin the paper to two pieces of fabric and carefully cut out the shape.

2 Make sure the patterned sides of fabric face each other.

Leave an opening at the top to allow for filling.

Sew around the shape 5mm (¼in) from the edge using backstitch.

Turn the shape right side out and fill. Work the filling in to all the corners and slip stitch (see page 54) to close the opening.

How to attach the mane

Insert the needle from the left and pull the yarn through but not all the way. Then insert the needle from the right and pull the yarn through to leave a loop.

Take the needle off the thread and adjust it so the ends are equal.

Stitch the tail to the pony.

Sew the ears either side of the head, and apply the eyes in the same way.

Thread the ends of the yarn through the loop and pull.

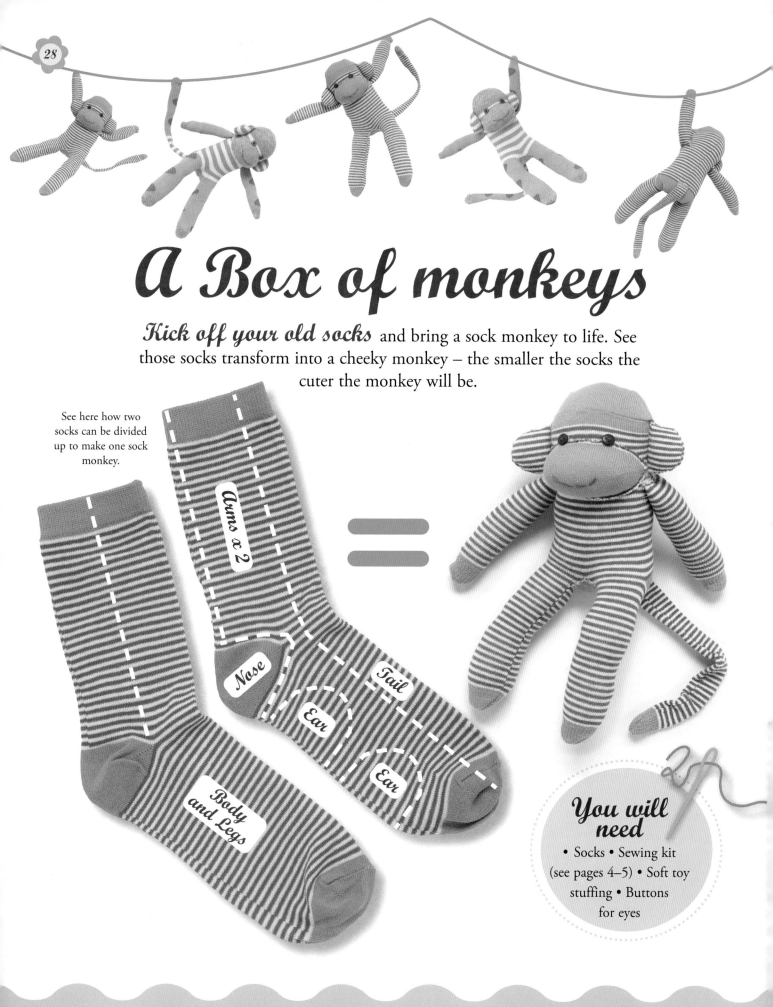

A Box of monkeys

Kick off your old socks and bring a sock monkey to life. See those socks transform into a cheeky monkey – the smaller the socks the cuter the monkey will be.

See here how two socks can be divided up to make one sock monkey.

Arms x 2

Nose

Ear

Tail

Ear

Body and Legs

=

You will need

• Socks • Sewing kit (see pages 4–5) • Soft toy stuffing • Buttons for eyes

Large or small socks?

Have fun using old or new socks to make your monkeys. Try tiny socks for babies, small socks for children, and big ones for adults.

How to make a Monkey

Body and legs

1

Turn the socks inside out and lay them flat with one heel facing forward.

Use backstitch (see page 54) to stitch from the heal down and around as shown.

Cut along the centre of the stitching to form the legs.

Tail, arms, nose, and ears

2

Cut out the body pieces in the places as shown on page 28.

Join the sides by stitching along the edges using overstitch (see page 54), leaving openings for stuffing.

Sew in a semicircle for the ears.

Ready to fill

3

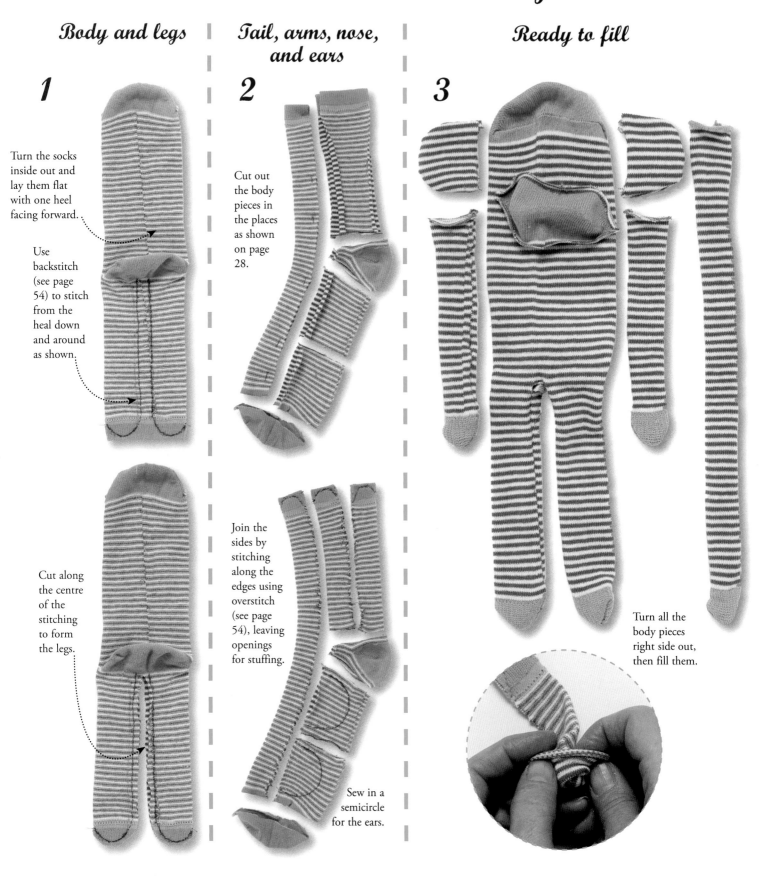

Turn all the body pieces right side out, then fill them.

Attach the ears and arms to the body.

Large and small monkeys

These monkeys are made from large and small socks. The small socks certainly make cuter and cuddly-looking toys.

Sew up the openings to the ears.

Sew up the body opening using overstitch.

Make a mouth

Sew on the bottom of the mouth.

Fill the mouth and attach the rest of the mouth.

Make eyes, a smile, and a tail

Sew on the button eyes.

Make a smile with embroidery thread using backstitch (see page 54).

Sew the tail to the base of the monkey's back.

Bunny girls

Rag-doll rabbits — here is a crafty twist on the classic rag doll. Dress these girls up and create their own fashion collection.

You will need

- Cotton fabric for each doll, 30cm x 60cm (12 x 24in) • Sewing kit (see pages 4–5) • Soft toy filling • Patterned cotton fabric for dress, 40cm x 25cm (16in x 10in) • Felt for eyes • Rickrack and ribbon

The bunnies get together for a tea party

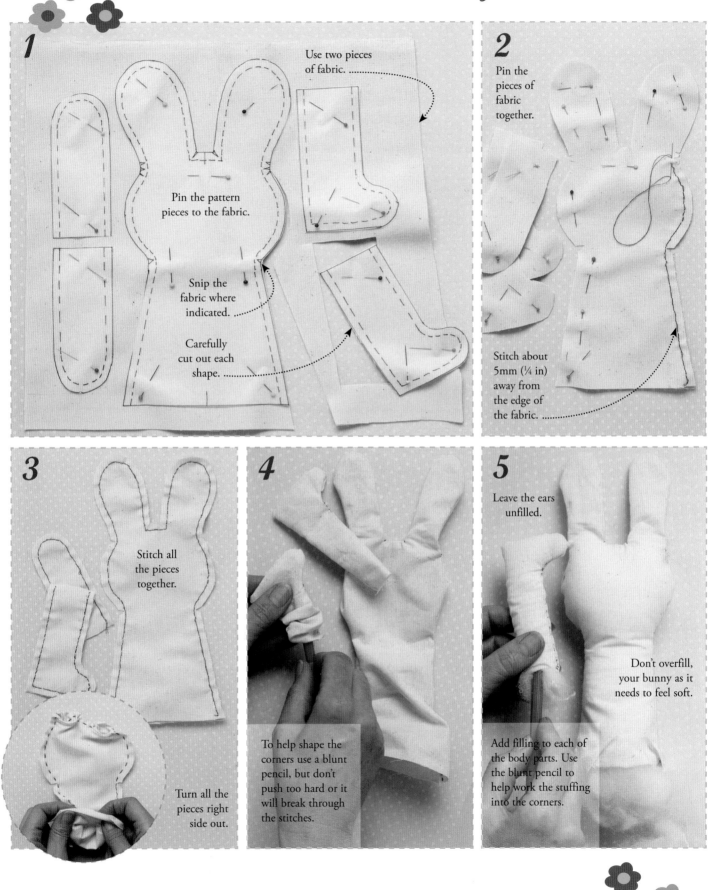

1

Use two pieces of fabric.

Pin the pattern pieces to the fabric.

Snip the fabric where indicated.

Carefully cut out each shape.

2

Pin the pieces of fabric together.

Stitch about 5mm (¼ in) away from the edge of the fabric.

3

Stitch all the pieces together.

Turn all the pieces right side out.

4

To help shape the corners use a blunt pencil, but don't push too hard or it will break through the stitches.

5

Leave the ears unfilled.

Don't overfill, your bunny as it needs to feel soft.

Add filling to each of the body parts. Use the blunt pencil to help work the stuffing into the corners.

Snip the fabric at these notches. It will help to shape the bunny when it is turned inside out.

Right leg x 2

The dotted lines show where to stitch.

Left leg x 2

Bunny's body

Lay tracing paper over the page and carefully draw over all the lines including the dotted ones. Cut out the paper shapes and use as your pattern. For more about templates turn to the back of the book.

Body x 2

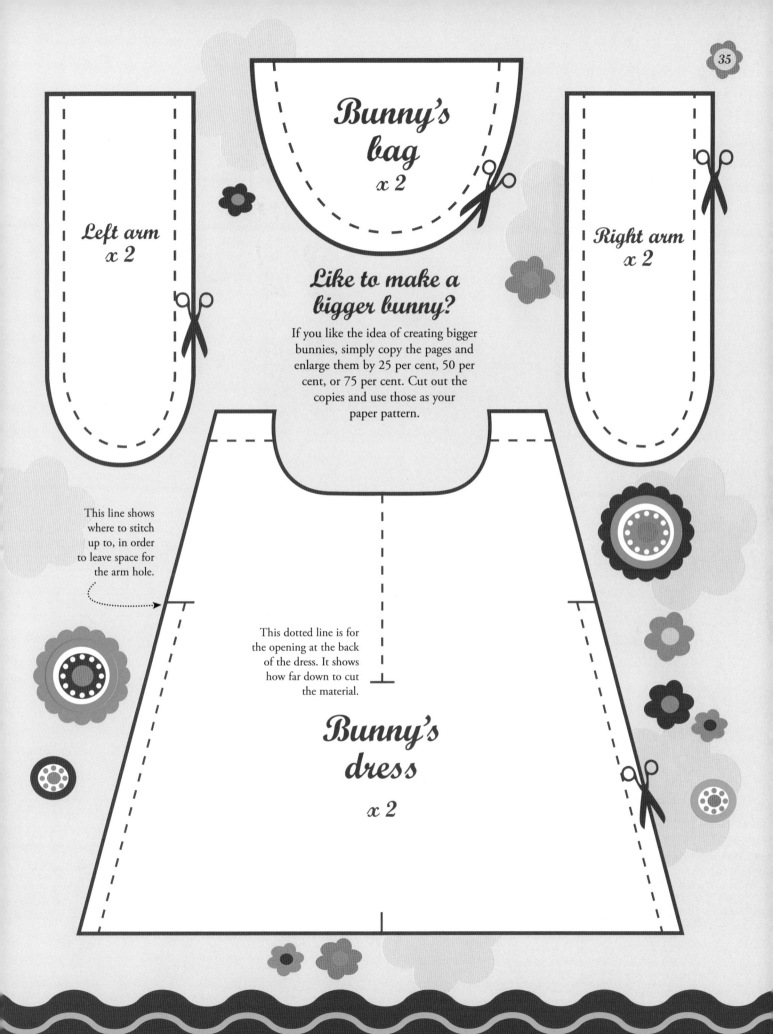

Bunny's bag
x 2

Left arm
x 2

Right arm
x 2

Like to make a bigger bunny?

If you like the idea of creating bigger bunnies, simply copy the pages and enlarge them by 25 per cent, 50 per cent, or 75 per cent. Cut out the copies and use those as your paper pattern.

This line shows where to stitch up to, in order to leave space for the arm hole.

This dotted line is for the opening at the back of the dress. It shows how far down to cut the material.

Bunny's dress

x 2

Prepare all the body pieces ready to assemble.

Putting Bunny together

Make Bunny's ears more shapely by pinching them in.

Sew a few stitches to hold in place.

Pin the back of the ears.

Attach felt eyes and sew bead in the middle.

Stitch on a nose and mouth. Work the stitches backwards and forwards to form the shape.

Fold the edge of the fabric over.

Close the end of the arm so the seams are together.

Neatly sew along the opening and attach the arms to the body.

Fold the edge of the fabric in and pin opening together.

Neatly sew the two edges together.

Back of doll

Turn the doll over and neatly stitch the legs to the body in overstitch (see page 54).

How to make bunny's dress and bag

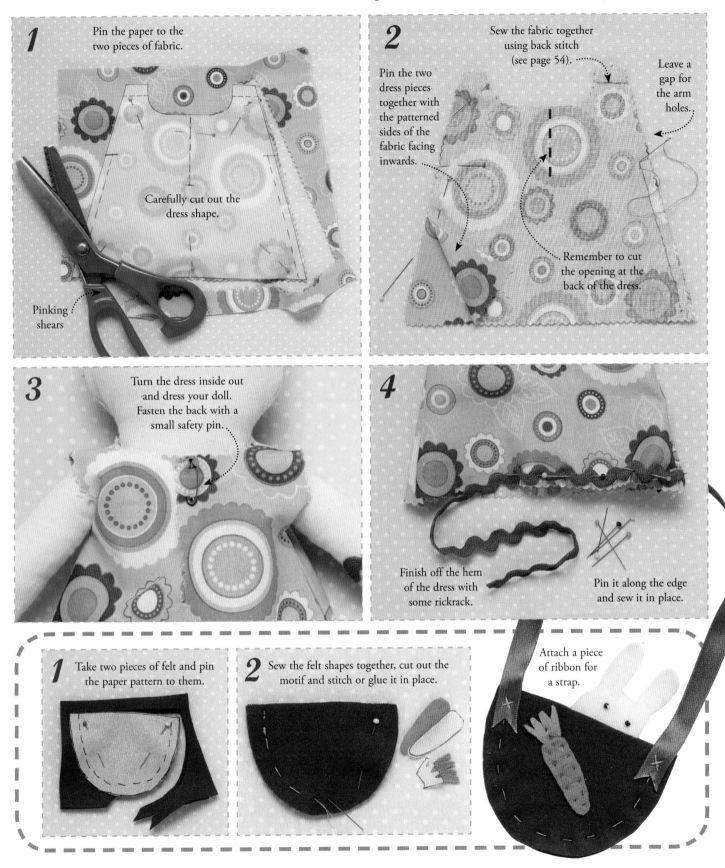

1 Pin the paper to the two pieces of fabric.

Carefully cut out the dress shape.

Pinking shears

2 Sew the fabric together using back stitch (see page 54).

Pin the two dress pieces together with the patterned sides of the fabric facing inwards.

Leave a gap for the arm holes.

Remember to cut the opening at the back of the dress.

3 Turn the dress inside out and dress your doll. Fasten the back with a small safety pin.

4 Finish off the hem of the dress with some rickrack.

Pin it along the edge and sew it in place.

1 Take two pieces of felt and pin the paper pattern to them.

2 Sew the felt shapes together, cut out the motif and stitch or glue it in place.

Attach a piece of ribbon for a strap.

Minimals

What do you call a tiny animal?

A minimal! These plumped up little cushions are not much bigger than your thumb.

You will need

- Colourful scraps of felt • Soft toy stuffing • Embroidery thread

Pin the template (see page 64) to the felt.

Body x 2

Eyes x 2

Tail x 1

Decorate the front first.

Use embroidery thread to add features.

Using sewing thread, stitch the front and back together.

Fill the tiny body with a small amount of filling.

Finish off by sewing up the base.

Little boxes of Minimals

Empty matchboxes make ideal places to keep your miniature animals. Decorate the boxes with matching fabric and give them away as gifts.

Boxes of minimals

We also make brilliant brooches.

Doodlephants

Who can resist a doodle?

This project combines a soft toy and a doodled design inspired by the medallions and flowers used on Indian fabrics. First make a plain elephant then doodle away.

Draw out your design directly on to the fabric.

Use felt for the ears and tail.

Permanent markers

Pens to use

You don't need special fabric pens for this project. Permanent markers will work just as well.

Cut the end of the tail into thin strips.

Calico or pale coloured cotton fabric will show up your doodles really well.

You will need

Cotton fabric such as calico for elephant body 60cm x 25cm (24in x 10in) • Grey felt for tail and ears • Sewing kit (see pages 4–5) • Permanent marker pens • Soft toy filling • Buttons for eyes

How to make an elephant

Follow the steps on the next page.

1

Fill the area with your design, leaving spaces that can be coloured in.

2

Now colour in your design.

3 **Finished colouring?**

The great thing about doodling is that the design is endless. There's always a little space that you can fill with a dot or a swirl.

Complete both sides of your elephant.

Find the pattern for Doodlephants on page 62

Make a plain elephant

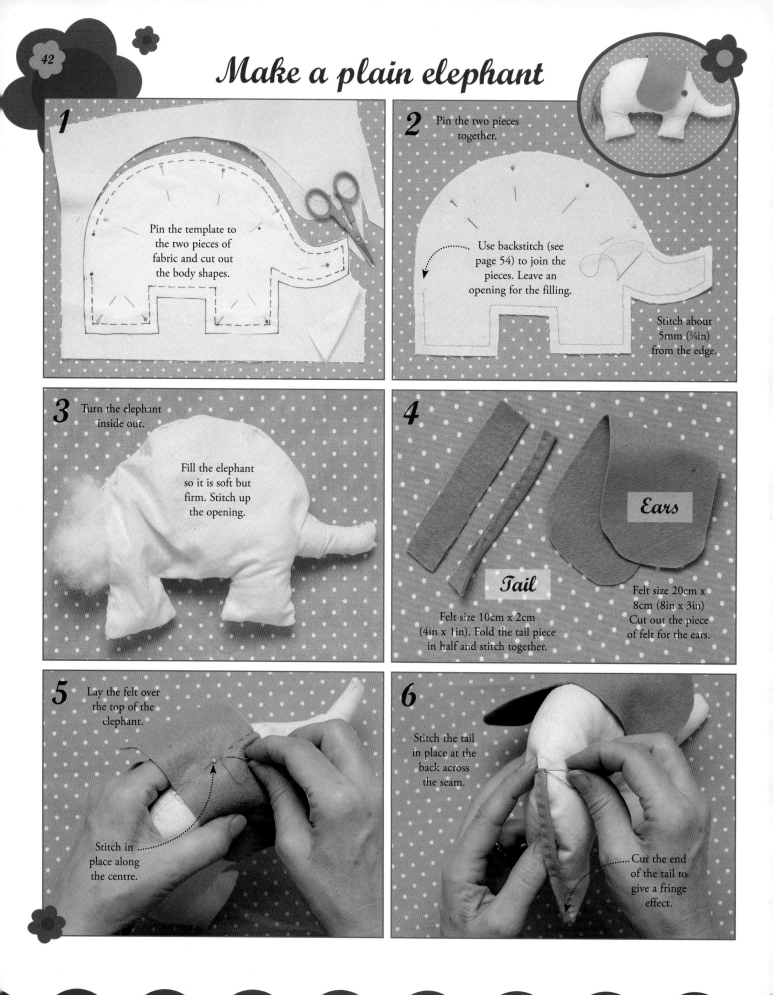

1 Pin the template to the two pieces of fabric and cut out the body shapes.

2 Pin the two pieces together.

Use backstitch (see page 54) to join the pieces. Leave an opening for the filling.

Stitch about 5mm (¼in) from the edge.

3 Turn the elephant inside out.

Fill the elephant so it is soft but firm. Stitch up the opening.

4

Tail

Felt size 10cm x 2cm (4in x 1in). Fold the tail piece in half and stitch together.

Ears

Felt size 20cm x 8cm (8in x 3in) Cut out the piece of felt for the ears.

5 Lay the felt over the top of the elephant.

Stitch in place along the centre.

6 Stitch the tail in place at the back across the seam.

Cut the end of the tail to give a fringe effect.

Cotton fabric

These elephants are made out of cotton calico. This is a cheap and versatile fabric. If you can't get hold of it try a plain pale-coloured cotton fabric.

Spring chickens

Make flocks of colourful birds. This busy clutch of chicks are made from colourful scraps of felt. Their wire legs give each one its own individual character.

You will need
- Colourful felt • 1m (3ft) plastic covered wire • Soft toy stuffing
- Embroidery thread
- Sewing kit (see pages 4–5)

How to make a chick

1

Attach the template (see page 47) to the felt pieces.

Body x 2

Wing x 2

2

With embroidery thread use running stitch (see page 54) to sew the body together.

Pin the two felt body shapes together.

Leave an opening for the filling.

Chicken legs

Take a strip of wire and bend it at the 18cm (7 in) point to form the beginning of the bird's foot.

Bend the wire backwards and forwards to form the claws.

Bend the wire to begin the next leg.

Wind the first piece of wire around the long length to form the first leg.

Repeat the steps to form the second leg.

Wind the last length of wire around the leg to finish off.

If you have too much wire left over, snip it off with scissors.

cheep cheep

3

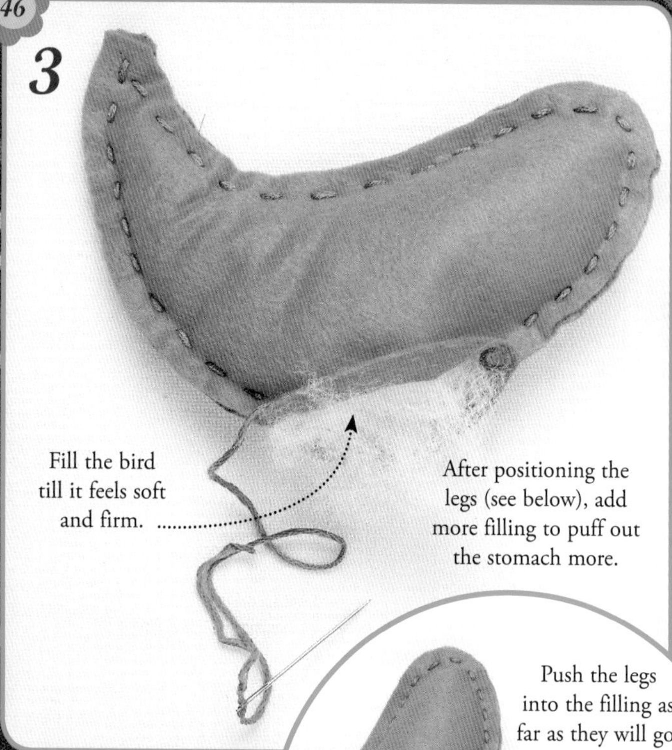

Fill the bird
till it feels soft
and firm.

After positioning the
legs (see below), add
more filling to puff out
the stomach more.

4

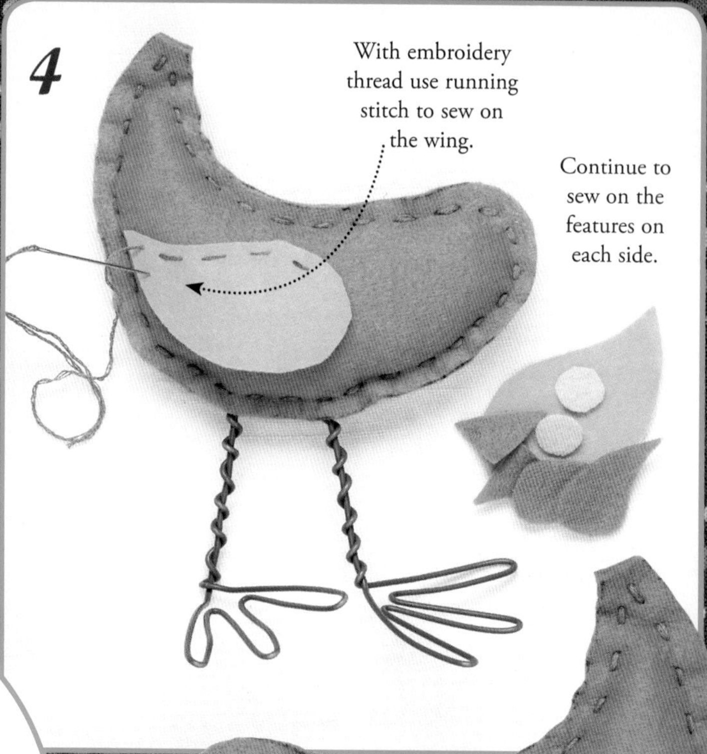

With embroidery
thread use running
stitch to sew on
the wing.

Continue to
sew on the
features on
each side.

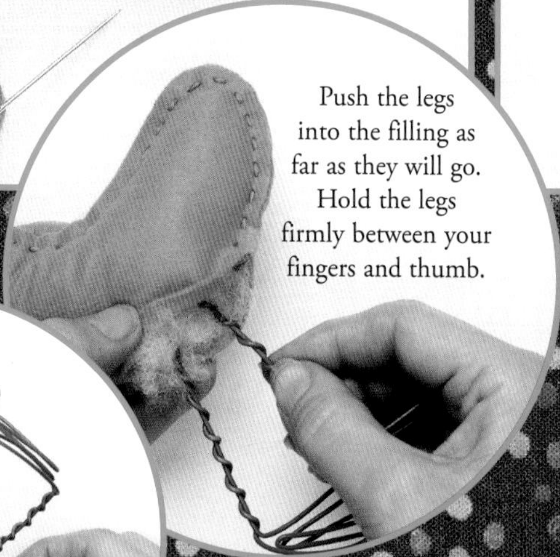

Push the legs
into the filling as
far as they will go.
Hold the legs
firmly between your
fingers and thumb.

Sew up the
opening,
stitching tightly
aroung the legs.

Bend the feet
at the ankle.

Adjust the
angle of the feet
so the bird stands up.

*chirp
chirp*

Get the chicken shape

A simple body shape echoed in the wings, and finished off with a beady eye and triangular beak. Try using lots of contrasting colours.

Jolly the Giraffe

Jolly and Jill the giraffes are standing tall – they can easily stand up for themselves with this simple design and require no complicated shaping.

Lovely legs

For your giraffe, choose some fun fabric like Jolly's which looks very giraffe-like. For an extra special effect use a contrasting fabric for the inside of your giraffe's legs.

You will need

• Cotton fabric 2 pieces 30cm x 30cm (12in x 12in) for the main body colour and 20cm x 24cm (8in x 9½in) contrasting colour for the inside of the legs
• Buttons for eyes and to attach the legs • Felt for tails and ears
• Soft toy filling • Sewing kit (see pages 4–5)

Find the pattern for jolly giraffes on page 63

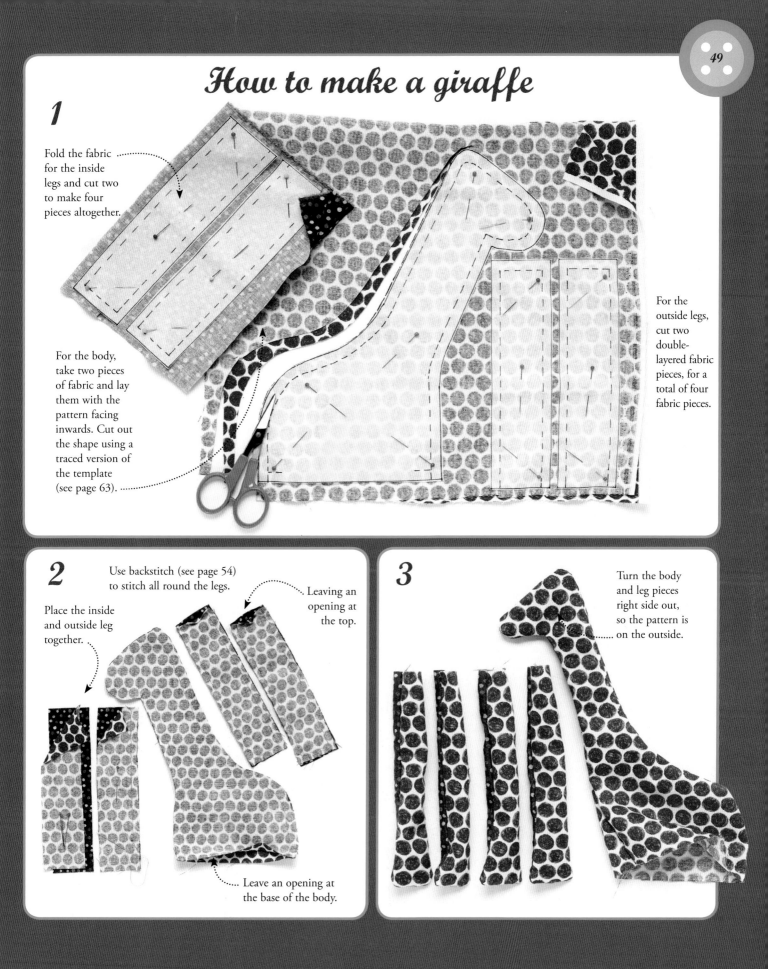

How to make a giraffe

1

Fold the fabric for the inside legs and cut two to make four pieces altogether.

For the body, take two pieces of fabric and lay them with the pattern facing inwards. Cut out the shape using a traced version of the template (see page 63).

For the outside legs, cut two double-layered fabric pieces, for a total of four fabric pieces.

2

Use backstitch (see page 54) to stitch all round the legs.

Place the inside and outside leg together.

Leaving an opening at the top.

Leave an opening at the base of the body.

3

Turn the body and leg pieces right side out, so the pattern is on the outside.

4

Fill all the body parts so they are soft but firm. ......

Work the stuffing evenly into the head and neck.

5

To finish off the legs, neatly fold the top of the fabric over and pin opening together. ......

Neatly sew up the opening in slipstitch (see page 54).

6

Fold in the edges of the fabric ...... and stitch up the opening using slipstitch.

Giraffes on the move

Because the legs are stitched on to the body separately they will move independently. This means you can put your giraffe into all sorts of poses.

Put the giraffe pieces together

Shaping the body

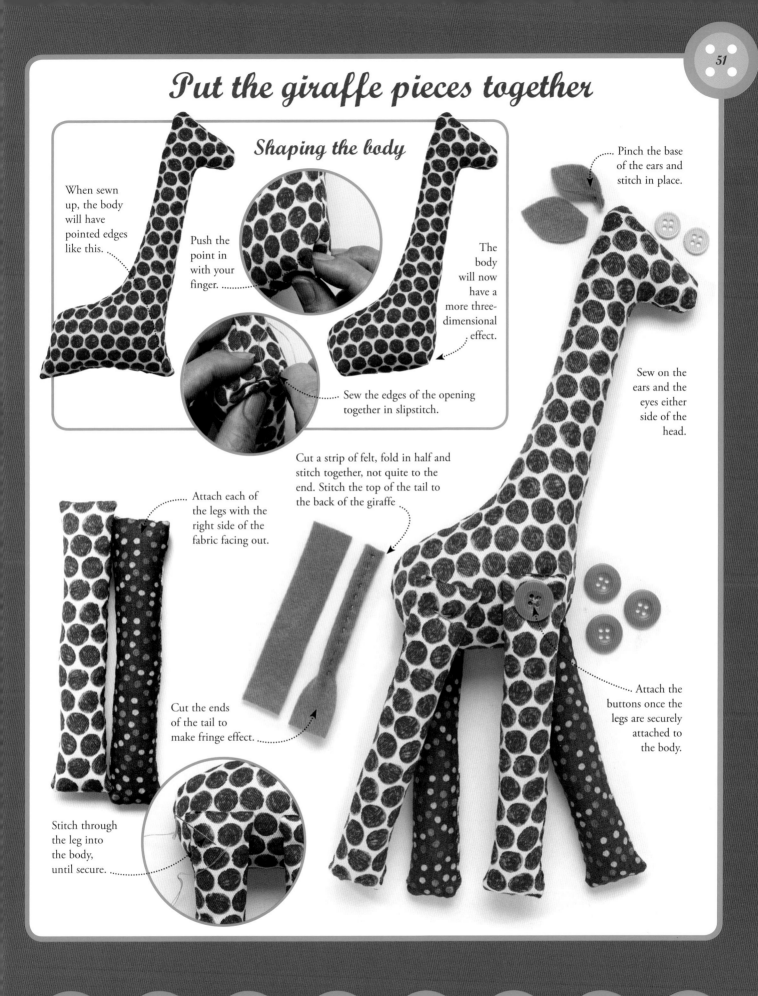

When sewn up, the body will have pointed edges like this.

Push the point in with your finger.

Sew the edges of the opening together in slipstitch.

The body will now have a more three-dimensional effect.

... Pinch the base of the ears and stitch in place.

Sew on the ears and the eyes either side of the head.

Attach each of the legs with the right side of the fabric facing out.

Cut a strip of felt, fold in half and stitch together, not quite to the end. Stitch the top of the tail to the back of the giraffe

Cut the ends of the tail to make fringe effect.

Attach the buttons once the legs are securely attached to the body.

Stitch through the leg into the body, until secure.

Mobile owls

Twirling and twisting – these mobiles work just as well on their own or in a group. Each owl is self-contained in its hoop.

You will need

- Felt for body a little smaller than the embroidery hoop • scraps of colourful felt for wings, feet and face • Sewing kit (see pages 4–5) • Soft toy stuffing • Buttons for eyes • length of cotton fabric or ribbon 1 metre (1¼yards) • Wooden embroidery hoop 14cm (5½in) • ribbon for hanging

Embroidery hoop
Choose a hoop big enough for your owl to swing freely.

How to make...
PAPER PATTERNS FROM THESE TEMPLATES
Lay tracing paper over the page and trace out the lines. Cut around the shape and pin the paper pattern to your fabric. See page 34 for more details.

Solid line
Cut fabric out along this line.

Wing

Wing

Feet

Template tip
To increase the size of the project – enlarge the pages on a photocopier or scanner.

How to make Owl

Prepare all the felt pieces using the template.

1 Take one body piece of felt and attach the features using overstitch (see page 54).

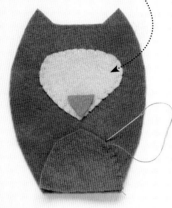

2 On the reverse, attach the wings and the feet.

Make the stitches neat and small.

3 Sew the front and back body pieces together.

Leave an opening at the base.

4

Fill the owl shape from the base and stitch shut.

5 Take a strip of patterned fabric 3cm (1in) wide and wrap it around the hoop. Hold it in place with a few stitches.

Wooden embroidery hoop.

6 Attach the owl by sewing a length of thread to the head and sew the other end to the fabric on the hoop.

The owl should swing freely in the hoop.

Tie a length of ribbon to the hoop and hang up the mobile.

How to stitch

Here are the stitches that are used for the projects. They all have a different job to do when you are joining fabric together for cushions, bags, and patchwork pieces.

How to start and finish

Begin stitching with a knot at the end of the thread. To end a row of stitches, make a tiny stitch, but do not pull it tight. Bring the thread back up through the loop and pull tight. Do this once more in the same spot, then cut the thread.

Running stitch

This is a very versatile stitch used for seams, joining fabric together, and for gathering.

Keep the stitch and the spaces between them small and even.

Backstitch

This is the strongest stitch. It makes a continuous line of stitches so it is best for joining two pieces of fabric securely, like the sides of a bag.

Make the stitch then bring the needle back to the place where the last stitch is finished.

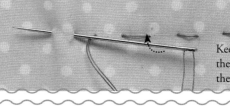
VIEW FROM REVERSE

Bring the needle out ready to begin the next stitch.

Tacking stitch

This is a temporary stitch. It will be removed but it is useful for holding pieces of fabric in place before you sew them together properly. It is also known as a basting stitch.

Tacking stitches are like running stitches but are larger and don't need to be even.

Overstitch

These are tiny, neat, and even stitches that are almost invisible. Use them to top sew two finished edges together, such as when you are joining patchwork pieces.

Insert the needle diagonally from the back of the fabric.

Pick up only two or three threads of fabric.

Slip stitch

Use slip stitch when you want the stitches to be invisible. This stitch is made by slipping the thread under a fold of fabric. It is often used to join two folded edges, such as the openings of cushions.

Slide the needle into the fold of the fabric.

Bring the needle out then slide the needle in the other side.

Lazy daisy stitch

This pretty stitch is very useful for embroidery decoration. Draw out your daisy design first in light pencil, then follow the lines with your stitches.

1. Tie a knot in your thread and pull it up through the beginning of a petal and down at the end.

2. Now bring it up through another petal until you have finished the flower.

Chain stitch

This is a very useful decorating stitch – great for flower stems and leaves. You may need to practise the stitch to get it just right.

1. Tie a knot in the thread and pull it up through the fabric.

2. Now push the needle back down next to the thread.

3. Don't pull it tight, leave a little loop.

4. Now bring the needle up through the loop and pull the thread through.

5. Repeat stages 1 to 4. Keep the stitches as even as possible.

Practise chain stitch on a curved line so you can make shapes.

Blanket stitch

This stitch is good for making neat, decorative edges and for sewing one piece of fabric to another.

1. Tie a knot in the thread and pull the needle up through the fabric.

2. Push the needle back through next to the stitch and up below it, making sure the loose end is caught as shown.

3. Push the needle down and up again so it is the same size as the previous stitch, catching the loose thread again.

4. Repeat these steps to make more loops.

Cross stitch

You can make whole pictures using cross-stitch.

1. Draw out crosses in light pencil on your fabric.

2. Sew a line of crosses from left to right in one direction...

... then finish them off by sewing back the other way.

Finishing off

On the back of the fabric, push the needle through the loop of the last stitch.

Pull the thread tight and repeat to make it secure.

Stitching tip

Try to keep your stitches even and neat.

Loops, called stitches

Rows

Ball of yarn

How to knit

From casting on to casting off –
Whether you are just learning or already have the knitting know-how, these pages are a handy reference.

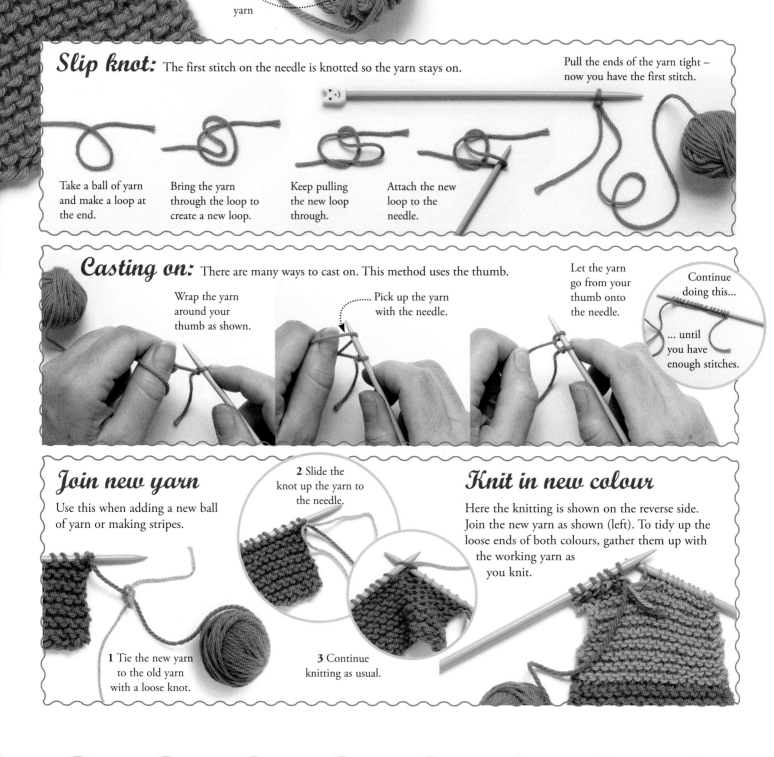

Slip knot: The first stitch on the needle is knotted so the yarn stays on.

Pull the ends of the yarn tight – now you have the first stitch.

Take a ball of yarn and make a loop at the end.

Bring the yarn through the loop to create a new loop.

Keep pulling the new loop through.

Attach the new loop to the needle.

Casting on: There are many ways to cast on. This method uses the thumb.

Wrap the yarn around your thumb as shown.

Pick up the yarn with the needle.

Let the yarn go from your thumb onto the needle.

Continue doing this... ... until you have enough stitches.

Join new yarn

Use this when adding a new ball of yarn or making stripes.

2 Slide the knot up the yarn to the needle.

1 Tie the new yarn to the old yarn with a loose knot.

3 Continue knitting as usual.

Knit in new colour

Here the knitting is shown on the reverse side. Join the new yarn as shown (left). To tidy up the loose ends of both colours, gather them up with the working yarn as you knit.

How many?

The projects in this book tell you how many stitches to cast on. Lots of stitches give you a wide fabric, while few stitches make a narrow fabric.

When you are starting a new row, start with the first stitch on the right and work towards the left.

The yarn will be on the right as well.

Getting started

You will need to cast on the number of stitches required in the pattern. The stitches that are being worked will be on the left hand needle and the ones you have made will go on the right.

Casting off

1 Begin the row by knitting two stitches.

2 Pick up the first stitch with the left needle.

3 Carry this first stitch over the second stitch and over the end of the needle.

4 Repeat steps 1–3...

5 ... until one stitch remains. Open up the loop

6 Cut the yarn and place the end in the loop.

7 Pull the yarn to close the loop.

Tidy away ends

Sewing in ends when adding new yarn or tidying the loose ends of finished pieces.

Use this method when tidying joined yarn and when knitting stripes.

Thread the end with a tapestry needle.

Sew the thread into the edge of the knitting.

Bring the needle out and cut the yarn.

Use this method when tidying loose ends of finished pieces.

Thread the needle onto the loose end and sew down the side of the knitting.

Bring the needle out and cut the yarn.

Knit stitch

Also called plain stitch — this is the most useful stitch. It's simple to make, and used in most projects – it's used to make Ted!

Garter Stitch

Garter stitch isn't an actual stitch but the name given to a piece of knitting where every row is knitted in knit stitch. The effect is bobbly on both sides.

Garter stitch is also made if you knit every row in purl stitch.

1 Hold the knitting with your hands in this position.

Take the yarn around the back.

Place the needle in the back of the stitch.

2 Wrap the yarn under and round the needle from right to left.

3 Pull on the yarn and move the needle from the back to the front.

4 The right needle is now on top of the left one and has taken the stitch with it.

5 Slide the top needle to the right. The stitch will now be transferred onto the right needle, completing the stitch.

Begin the next stitch as in step 1.

Purl stitch

Working from the front — This stitch is made by the needle going in the front of the stitch. It's when knit and purl stitch rows are alternated that the knitting looks smoth – just like the Knittens!

For purl stitch, the needle goes in the front of the stitch.

The yarn also goes at the front too.

1 Hold the knitting with your hands in this position. Bring the yarn to the front.

Place the needle in the front of the stitch.

2 Take the yarn between the needles.

3 Wrap it round the needle from right to left.

4 Pull on the yarn and move the needle from front to back ...

5 ... taking the stitch with it.

6 Take the rest of the yarn off the needle to complete the stitch.

Begin the next stitch as in step 1.

Purl stitch + Knit stitch = Stocking stitch

STOCKING STITCH isn't an actual stitch at all. Instead it is made by working a knit row then a purl row, a knit row then a purl row and so on. The result is a smooth front to the knitting and a "bobbly" back.

FRONT
The knit-stitch side

BACK
The purl-stitch side

Dog's best friends

'V' shapes
After sewing the two shapes together snip along these lines – it will help shaping the fabric.

Ear

Nose

Solid line
Cut fabric out along this line.

Fold line of he fabric

Dotted line
Stitch along this line.

Opening
Stitch to these dots to leave an opening for filling the toy.

How to make...
PAPER PATTERNS FROM THESE TEMPLATES
Lay tracing paper over the page and trace out the lines. Cut around the shape and pin the paper pattern to your fabric.
See page 34 for more details.

Tail

Template tip
To increase the size of the project, enlarge the pages on a photocopier or scanner.

Your little pony

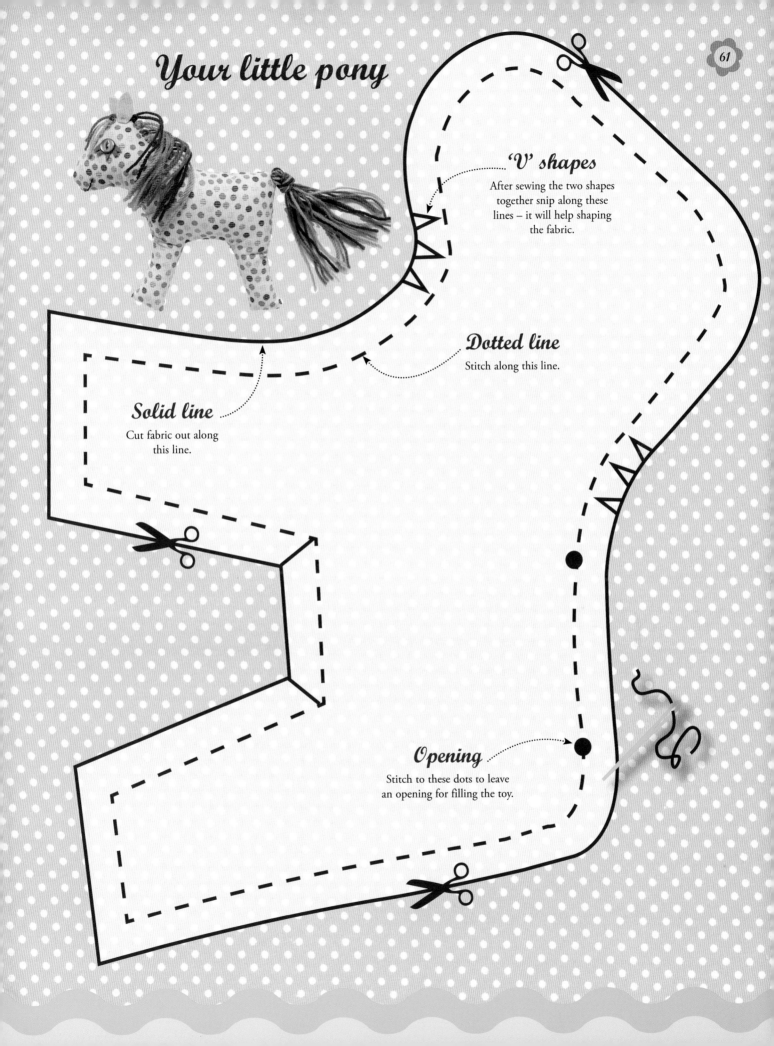

'V' shapes

After sewing the two shapes together snip along these lines – it will help shaping the fabric.

Dotted line

Stitch along this line.

Solid line

Cut fabric out along this line.

Opening

Stitch to these dots to leave an opening for filling the toy.

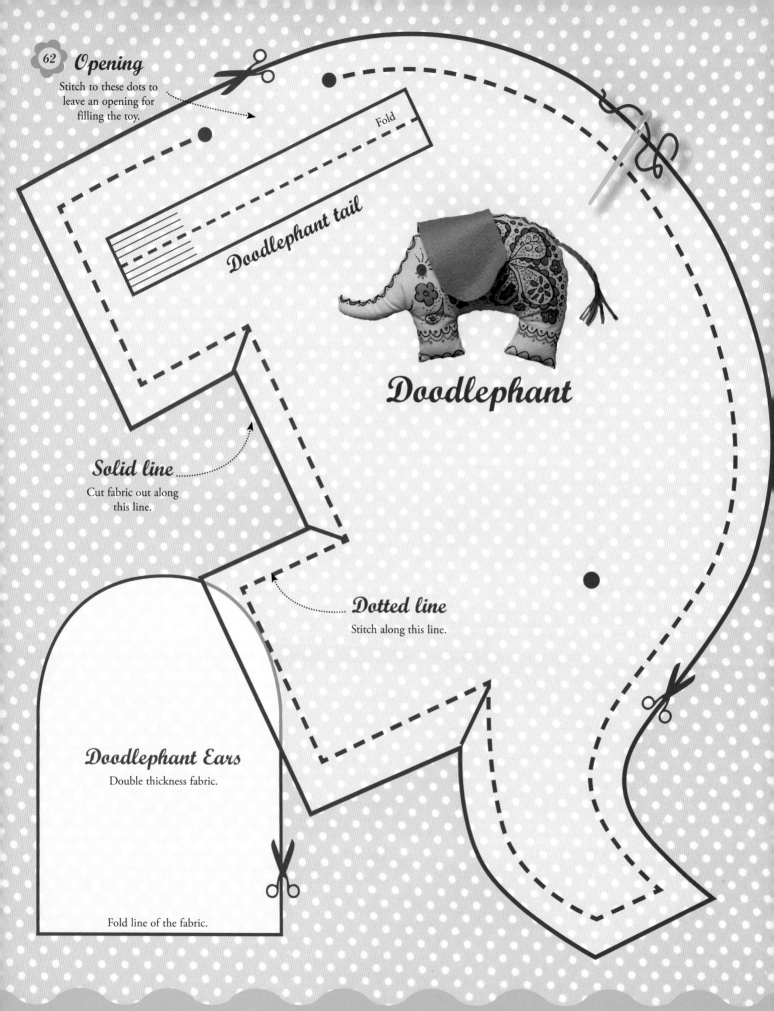

Opening

Stitch to these dots to leave an opening for filling the toy.

Fold

Doodlephant tail

Doodlephant

Solid line

Cut fabric out along this line.

Dotted line

Stitch along this line.

Doodlephant Ears

Double thickness fabric.

Fold line of the fabric.

Jolly the Giraffe

Dotted line
Stitch along this line.

Solid line
Cut fabric out along this line.

How to make...
A PAPER PATTERN FROM THIS TEMPLATE
Lay tracing paper over the page and trace out the lines. Cut around the shape and pin the paper pattern to your fabric.
See page 34 for more details.

Fold fabric on this line

Tail

Giraffe legs x 4
Double thickness fabric

Opening
Stitch to these dots to leave an opening for filling the toy.

Template tip
To increase the size of the project – enlarge the pages on a photocopier or scanner

Index